50 Wild Foods from Forest to Table

By: Kelly Johnson

Table of Contents

- Morel Mushrooms
- Chanterelle Mushrooms
- Chicken of the Woods
- Maitake (Hen of the Woods)
- Black Trumpet Mushrooms
- Oyster Mushrooms
- Stinging Nettle
- Dandelion Greens
- Wild Ramps (Wild Leeks)
- Fiddlehead Ferns
- Purslane
- Sorrel
- Wood Sorrel
- Lamb's Quarters
- Wild Garlic
- Wild Onions
- Burdock Root
- Cattail Shoots
- Acorns
- Black Walnuts
- Hickory Nuts
- Beech Nuts
- Pine Nuts
- Wild Hazelnuts
- Pawpaw Fruit
- Wild Persimmons
- Serviceberries (Juneberries)
- Elderberries
- Wild Blueberries
- Wild Strawberries
- Wild Raspberries
- Wild Blackberries
- Gooseberries
- Chokecherries
- Mulberries

- Autumn Olives
- Hawthorn Berries
- Rose Hips
- Sumac Berries
- Sassafras
- Wild Ginger
- Yarrow
- Chickweed
- Miner's Lettuce
- Watercress
- Thistle Root
- Cactus Fruit (Prickly Pear)
- Wild Mustard Greens
- Wild Asparagus
- Indian Cucumber Root

Sautéed Morel Mushrooms

Ingredients:

- ½ lb fresh morel mushrooms (or dried morels, rehydrated)
- 2 tbsp unsalted butter
- 1 tbsp olive oil
- 2 cloves garlic, minced
- 1 small shallot, finely chopped
- ¼ cup dry white wine (optional)
- 1 tsp fresh thyme (or ½ tsp dried)
- Salt and black pepper, to taste
- 1 tbsp fresh parsley, chopped
- 1 tbsp heavy cream (optional, for a creamy version)

Instructions:

1. **Clean the morels** – Slice them in half and soak in cold salt water for 15-20 minutes to remove dirt and insects. Rinse thoroughly and pat dry.
2. **Heat the pan** – In a large skillet over medium heat, melt the butter with olive oil.
3. **Sauté aromatics** – Add the minced garlic and chopped shallot, cooking until fragrant and softened (about 2 minutes).
4. **Cook the morels** – Add the morel mushrooms and sauté for 5-7 minutes until tender and slightly crispy on the edges.
5. **Deglaze the pan** (optional) – Pour in the white wine and let it cook down for 1-2 minutes, allowing the alcohol to evaporate.
6. **Season** – Stir in thyme, salt, and black pepper. If using, add the heavy cream and cook for another minute until creamy.
7. **Garnish & serve** – Sprinkle with fresh parsley and serve immediately.

Serving Suggestions:

- Enjoy as a side dish with steak, chicken, or fish.
- Serve over toasted bread, risotto, or pasta.
- Pair with scrambled eggs for a luxurious breakfast.

Sautéed Chanterelle Mushrooms

Ingredients:

- ½ lb fresh chanterelle mushrooms, cleaned and sliced
- 2 tbsp unsalted butter
- 1 tbsp olive oil
- 2 cloves garlic, minced
- 1 small shallot, finely chopped
- 1 tsp fresh thyme (or ½ tsp dried)
- Salt and black pepper, to taste
- 1 tbsp fresh parsley, chopped
- ¼ cup dry white wine (optional)

Instructions:

1. Heat butter and olive oil in a skillet over medium heat.
2. Add garlic and shallots, sautéing until soft and fragrant.
3. Add chanterelle mushrooms and cook for 5-7 minutes until tender.
4. Stir in thyme, salt, and black pepper. Add white wine if using and let it cook down.
5. Garnish with parsley and serve warm.

Crispy Chicken of the Woods

Ingredients:

- ½ lb Chicken of the Woods mushrooms, cut into strips
- ½ cup all-purpose flour
- ½ tsp salt
- ½ tsp black pepper
- ½ tsp smoked paprika
- 1 egg, beaten
- ½ cup breadcrumbs
- 2 tbsp olive oil or butter

Instructions:

1. In a bowl, mix flour, salt, pepper, and paprika.
2. Dip each mushroom strip into flour, then egg, then breadcrumbs.
3. Heat oil in a skillet over medium heat.
4. Fry mushrooms for 3-4 minutes per side until golden brown.
5. Drain on paper towels and serve warm.

Garlic Butter Maitake (Hen of the Woods)

Ingredients:

- ½ lb maitake mushrooms, cleaned and separated into pieces
- 2 tbsp unsalted butter
- 1 tbsp olive oil
- 2 cloves garlic, minced
- 1 tsp soy sauce
- ½ tsp fresh thyme
- Salt and black pepper, to taste

Instructions:

1. Heat butter and olive oil in a skillet over medium heat.
2. Add garlic and sauté until fragrant.
3. Add maitake mushrooms and cook for 5-7 minutes until crispy.
4. Stir in soy sauce, thyme, salt, and pepper.
5. Serve immediately as a side dish or topping.

Black Trumpet Mushroom Risotto

Ingredients:

- ½ cup dried or fresh black trumpet mushrooms
- 1 cup Arborio rice
- 4 cups vegetable or chicken broth, warmed
- ½ cup dry white wine
- 1 small onion, finely chopped
- 2 tbsp butter
- ¼ cup Parmesan cheese, grated
- Salt and black pepper, to taste

Instructions:

1. If using dried mushrooms, soak in warm water for 20 minutes, then drain.
2. Heat butter in a pan over medium heat and sauté onions until soft.
3. Add Arborio rice and toast for 1-2 minutes.
4. Pour in white wine and cook until absorbed.
5. Gradually add warm broth, stirring continuously, until rice is tender.
6. Stir in mushrooms, Parmesan cheese, salt, and pepper.
7. Serve warm and enjoy.

Garlic Butter Oyster Mushrooms

Ingredients:

- ½ lb oyster mushrooms, cleaned and torn into pieces
- 2 tbsp unsalted butter
- 1 tbsp olive oil
- 2 cloves garlic, minced
- 1 tsp soy sauce (optional)
- Salt and black pepper, to taste
- 1 tbsp fresh parsley, chopped

Instructions:

1. Heat butter and olive oil in a pan over medium heat.
2. Add garlic and sauté until fragrant.
3. Add oyster mushrooms and cook for 5-7 minutes until golden and crispy.
4. Stir in soy sauce, salt, and black pepper.
5. Garnish with parsley and serve warm.

Stinging Nettle Soup

Ingredients:

- 4 cups fresh stinging nettles (wear gloves while handling)
- 1 tbsp olive oil
- 1 small onion, chopped
- 2 cloves garlic, minced
- 1 medium potato, diced
- 4 cups vegetable broth
- ½ cup heavy cream (optional)
- Salt and black pepper, to taste

Instructions:

1. Blanch nettles in boiling water for 1 minute to remove the sting. Drain and chop.
2. Heat oil in a pot over medium heat, add onion and garlic, and sauté until soft.
3. Add potato and broth, bring to a boil, and simmer for 15 minutes.
4. Stir in nettles and cook for another 5 minutes.
5. Blend until smooth, season with salt and pepper, and stir in cream if using.
6. Serve warm.

Sautéed Dandelion Greens with Garlic

Ingredients:

- 4 cups dandelion greens, washed and chopped
- 1 tbsp olive oil
- 2 cloves garlic, minced
- ½ tsp red pepper flakes (optional)
- Salt and black pepper, to taste
- 1 tbsp lemon juice

Instructions:

1. Heat olive oil in a pan over medium heat.
2. Add garlic and red pepper flakes, sauté for 30 seconds.
3. Add dandelion greens and cook for 3-4 minutes until wilted.
4. Season with salt, pepper, and lemon juice.
5. Serve as a side dish.

Wild Ramps (Wild Leeks) Pesto

Ingredients:

- 1 cup wild ramps, chopped
- ¼ cup walnuts or pine nuts
- ½ cup Parmesan cheese, grated
- ½ cup olive oil
- Salt and black pepper, to taste
- Juice of ½ lemon

Instructions:

1. Blend ramps, nuts, and Parmesan in a food processor.
2. Slowly add olive oil while blending until smooth.
3. Season with salt, pepper, and lemon juice.
4. Serve over pasta or as a spread.

Sautéed Fiddlehead Ferns

Ingredients:

- 2 cups fiddlehead ferns, washed and trimmed
- 2 tbsp butter or olive oil
- 2 cloves garlic, minced
- Salt and black pepper, to taste
- 1 tbsp lemon juice

Instructions:

1. Blanch fiddleheads in boiling water for 5 minutes, then drain.
2. Heat butter in a pan, add garlic, and sauté for 1 minute.
3. Add fiddleheads and cook for 3-4 minutes until tender.
4. Season with salt, pepper, and lemon juice.
5. Serve warm.

Purslane Salad with Lemon Dressing

Ingredients:

- 2 cups fresh purslane, washed
- 1 small cucumber, sliced
- ½ cup cherry tomatoes, halved
- ¼ red onion, thinly sliced
- 2 tbsp olive oil
- 1 tbsp lemon juice
- Salt and black pepper, to taste

Instructions:

1. Toss purslane, cucumber, tomatoes, and onion in a bowl.
2. Whisk together olive oil, lemon juice, salt, and pepper.
3. Drizzle dressing over the salad and toss to coat.
4. Serve fresh.

Sorrel Soup

Ingredients:

- 2 cups fresh sorrel, chopped
- 1 tbsp butter
- 1 small onion, chopped
- 2 cups vegetable broth
- ½ cup heavy cream
- Salt and black pepper, to taste

Instructions:

1. Heat butter in a pot and sauté onion until soft.
2. Add sorrel and cook until wilted.
3. Pour in broth, bring to a simmer, and cook for 10 minutes.
4. Blend until smooth, stir in cream, and season with salt and pepper.
5. Serve warm.

Wood Sorrel Lemonade

Ingredients:

- 1 cup fresh wood sorrel leaves
- 4 cups water
- ¼ cup honey or sugar
- Juice of 2 lemons

Instructions:

1. Blend wood sorrel and water together, then strain.
2. Stir in honey or sugar until dissolved.
3. Add lemon juice and mix well.
4. Serve chilled over ice.

Sautéed Lamb's Quarters with Garlic

Ingredients:

- 4 cups lamb's quarters, washed
- 1 tbsp olive oil
- 2 cloves garlic, minced
- Salt and black pepper, to taste

Instructions:

1. Heat olive oil in a pan over medium heat.
2. Add garlic and sauté for 1 minute.
3. Add lamb's quarters and cook for 3-4 minutes until wilted.
4. Season with salt and pepper.
5. Serve as a side dish.

Wild Garlic Butter

Ingredients:

- ½ cup wild garlic, chopped
- 1 stick unsalted butter, softened
- ½ tsp salt

Instructions:

1. Mash butter with wild garlic and salt until combined.
2. Roll into a log and refrigerate until firm.
3. Slice and use on bread, meat, or vegetables.

Wild Onion and Cheese Omelet

Ingredients:

- 2 eggs
- ¼ cup wild onions, chopped
- ¼ cup shredded cheese (cheddar or Swiss)
- 1 tbsp butter
- Salt and black pepper, to taste

Instructions:

1. Beat eggs with salt and pepper.
2. Melt butter in a pan, add wild onions, and sauté for 1 minute.
3. Pour eggs into the pan and cook until set.
4. Sprinkle cheese on top, fold the omelet, and serve warm.

Sautéed Burdock Root with Sesame

Ingredients:

- 1 burdock root, peeled and julienned
- 1 tbsp sesame oil
- 2 cloves garlic, minced
- 1 tbsp soy sauce
- 1 tsp honey
- 1 tsp sesame seeds

Instructions:

1. Soak burdock root in water for 10 minutes to remove bitterness. Drain.
2. Heat sesame oil in a pan over medium heat.
3. Add burdock root and garlic, sauté for 5 minutes.
4. Stir in soy sauce and honey, cook for another 2 minutes.
5. Sprinkle sesame seeds before serving.

Cattail Shoots Stir-Fry

Ingredients:

- 2 cups cattail shoots, sliced
- 1 tbsp olive oil
- 1 small onion, chopped
- 2 cloves garlic, minced
- ½ tsp salt
- Black pepper, to taste

Instructions:

1. Heat oil in a pan over medium heat.
2. Add onion and garlic, sauté until fragrant.
3. Add cattail shoots, stir-fry for 3-4 minutes until tender.
4. Season with salt and pepper.
5. Serve warm as a side dish.

Roasted Acorn Flour Pancakes

Ingredients:

- 1 cup acorn flour
- ½ cup all-purpose flour
- 1 tsp baking powder
- ½ tsp salt
- 1 egg
- 1 cup milk
- 1 tbsp honey

Instructions:

1. Mix dry ingredients in a bowl.
2. In another bowl, whisk egg, milk, and honey.
3. Combine wet and dry ingredients.
4. Heat a pan over medium heat and cook pancakes until golden brown.
5. Serve with maple syrup or wild berries.

Black Walnut Maple Cookies

Ingredients:

- 1 cup butter, softened
- ¾ cup brown sugar
- 1 egg
- 1 tsp vanilla extract
- 2 cups flour
- ½ tsp salt
- 1 cup chopped black walnuts
- ¼ cup maple syrup

Instructions:

1. Preheat oven to 350°F (175°C).
2. Cream butter and sugar, then mix in egg and vanilla.
3. Add flour, salt, and mix until combined.
4. Stir in black walnuts and maple syrup.
5. Drop spoonfuls onto a baking sheet and bake for 10-12 minutes.

Hickory Nut Butter

Ingredients:

- 2 cups hickory nuts, shelled
- 1 tbsp honey
- 1 tbsp olive oil
- Pinch of salt

Instructions:

1. Toast hickory nuts in a dry pan over medium heat for 5 minutes.
2. Blend nuts in a food processor until smooth.
3. Add honey, olive oil, and salt. Blend again.
4. Store in a jar and spread on toast or fruit.

Roasted Beech Nuts

Ingredients:

- 1 cup beech nuts, shelled
- 1 tbsp butter
- ½ tsp salt

Instructions:

1. Preheat oven to 325°F (163°C).
2. Toss beech nuts with melted butter and salt.
3. Spread on a baking sheet and roast for 10-12 minutes until golden.
4. Enjoy as a snack.

Pine Nut Pesto

Ingredients:

- ½ cup pine nuts
- 2 cups fresh basil
- ½ cup Parmesan cheese
- 2 cloves garlic
- ½ cup olive oil
- Salt and black pepper, to taste

Instructions:

1. Toast pine nuts in a dry pan for 2-3 minutes.
2. Blend basil, Parmesan, garlic, and pine nuts.
3. Slowly add olive oil while blending until smooth.
4. Season with salt and pepper. Serve with pasta or bread.

Wild Hazelnut Chocolate Spread

Ingredients:

- 1 cup wild hazelnuts, toasted
- ¼ cup cocoa powder
- ¼ cup honey or maple syrup
- 1 tbsp coconut oil
- ½ tsp vanilla extract
- Pinch of salt

Instructions:

1. Blend hazelnuts in a food processor until smooth.
2. Add cocoa, honey, coconut oil, vanilla, and salt. Blend again.
3. Store in a jar and use as a spread.

Pawpaw Pudding

Ingredients:

- 1 cup pawpaw pulp
- ½ cup sugar
- 2 eggs
- ½ cup milk
- 1 tsp vanilla extract
- ½ cup flour
- ½ tsp baking powder

Instructions:

1. Preheat oven to 350°F (175°C).
2. Mix pawpaw pulp, sugar, eggs, milk, and vanilla.
3. Stir in flour and baking powder.
4. Pour into a greased baking dish and bake for 30-35 minutes.
5. Serve warm or chilled.

Wild Persimmon Bread

Ingredients:

- 1 cup wild persimmon pulp
- ½ cup sugar
- 2 eggs
- ½ cup butter, melted
- 1 ½ cups flour
- 1 tsp baking soda
- ½ tsp cinnamon
- ¼ tsp salt

Instructions:

1. Preheat oven to 350°F (175°C).
2. Mix persimmon pulp, sugar, eggs, and butter.
3. Stir in dry ingredients until combined.
4. Pour batter into a greased loaf pan.
5. Bake for 50-60 minutes.
6. Cool before slicing.

Serviceberry (Juneberry) Jam

Ingredients:

- 2 cups serviceberries (Juneberries)
- 1 cup sugar or honey
- 1 tbsp lemon juice
- ½ cup water

Instructions:

1. Rinse serviceberries and remove stems.
2. Combine berries, sugar, lemon juice, and water in a saucepan.
3. Simmer over medium heat for 15-20 minutes, stirring occasionally.
4. Mash the berries and cook until the jam thickens.
5. Pour into sterilized jars and let cool before refrigerating.

Elderberry Syrup

Ingredients:

- 2 cups fresh elderberries (or 1 cup dried)
- 4 cups water
- 1 cup honey
- 1 cinnamon stick (optional)

Instructions:

1. Simmer elderberries and water in a pot for 30 minutes.
2. Mash berries, then strain through a cheesecloth.
3. Return liquid to the pot and add honey.
4. Stir well and store in a sealed jar.
5. Use as a syrup for pancakes, teas, or medicinal remedies.

Wild Blueberry Muffins

Ingredients:

- 1 ½ cups wild blueberries
- 2 cups flour
- ¾ cup sugar
- 2 tsp baking powder
- ½ tsp salt
- 1 egg
- ¾ cup milk
- ⅓ cup butter, melted

Instructions:

1. Preheat oven to 375°F (190°C).
2. Mix flour, sugar, baking powder, and salt in a bowl.
3. In another bowl, whisk egg, milk, and butter.
4. Combine wet and dry ingredients, then fold in blueberries.
5. Fill muffin cups and bake for 20-25 minutes.

Wild Strawberry & Mint Salad

Ingredients:

- 2 cups wild strawberries
- 1 tbsp honey
- 1 tbsp fresh mint, chopped
- 1 tsp lemon juice

Instructions:

1. Rinse wild strawberries and slice in half.
2. Toss with honey, lemon juice, and mint.
3. Chill for 10 minutes and serve as a refreshing salad.

Wild Raspberry Vinaigrette

Ingredients:

- 1 cup wild raspberries
- ¼ cup olive oil
- 2 tbsp balsamic vinegar
- 1 tbsp honey
- ½ tsp salt
- ¼ tsp black pepper

Instructions:

1. Blend all ingredients until smooth.
2. Strain if desired for a smoother texture.
3. Drizzle over salads or roasted vegetables.

Wild Blackberry Cobbler

Ingredients:

- 3 cups wild blackberries
- ½ cup sugar
- 1 tbsp lemon juice
- 1 cup flour
- 1 cup milk
- ½ cup butter, melted
- 1 tsp baking powder

Instructions:

1. Preheat oven to 375°F (190°C).
2. Toss blackberries with sugar and lemon juice.
3. Mix flour, milk, melted butter, and baking powder to form a batter.
4. Pour batter into a greased baking dish and top with blackberries.
5. Bake for 30-35 minutes until golden brown.

Gooseberry Pie

Ingredients:

- 3 cups gooseberries, washed and trimmed
- 1 cup sugar
- 2 tbsp cornstarch
- 1 tsp lemon zest
- 1 tbsp butter, cut into small pieces
- 1 prepared pie crust

Instructions:

1. Preheat oven to 375°F (190°C).
2. Mix gooseberries, sugar, cornstarch, and lemon zest.
3. Pour into the pie crust and dot with butter.
4. Cover with a second crust or lattice top, sealing edges.
5. Bake for 40-45 minutes until golden brown.

Chokecherry Jelly

Ingredients:

- 4 cups chokecherries, stemmed
- 4 cups water
- 4 cups sugar
- 1 package (1.75 oz) pectin

Instructions:

1. Boil chokecherries and water for 20 minutes, then strain.
2. Return juice to pot, add pectin, and bring to a boil.
3. Stir in sugar and boil for 2 more minutes.
4. Pour into sterilized jars and seal.

Mulberry Pancakes

Ingredients:

- 1 cup mulberries
- 1 cup flour
- 1 tbsp sugar
- 1 tsp baking powder
- ½ tsp salt
- 1 cup milk
- 1 egg
- 1 tbsp butter, melted

Instructions:

1. Mix flour, sugar, baking powder, and salt.
2. Whisk in milk, egg, and melted butter.
3. Fold in mulberries.
4. Cook pancakes on a hot griddle until golden brown.

Autumn Olive Fruit Leather

Ingredients:

- 3 cups autumn olives, washed
- ¼ cup honey
- ½ tsp cinnamon

Instructions:

1. Blend autumn olives into a purée.
2. Strain out seeds and mix in honey and cinnamon.
3. Spread on a baking sheet lined with parchment paper.
4. Bake at 170°F (75°C) for 6-8 hours until dry.

Hawthorn Berry Tea

Ingredients:

- 1 cup dried hawthorn berries
- 4 cups water
- 1 cinnamon stick (optional)
- 1 tbsp honey

Instructions:

1. Simmer hawthorn berries and water for 20 minutes.
2. Strain and sweeten with honey.
3. Serve warm.

Rose Hip Syrup

Ingredients:

- 2 cups rose hips, cleaned and chopped
- 4 cups water
- 1 cup sugar or honey

Instructions:

1. Simmer rose hips in water for 30 minutes.
2. Strain, then return liquid to pot.
3. Stir in sugar or honey until dissolved.
4. Store in the fridge and use in drinks or desserts.

Sumac Lemonade

Ingredients:

- 5 sumac berry clusters
- 4 cups water
- 2 tbsp honey or sugar
- Ice and lemon slices for serving

Instructions:

1. Soak sumac berries in water for 4 hours.
2. Strain through a fine mesh or cheesecloth.
3. Stir in honey or sugar and serve over ice.

Sassafras Tea

Ingredients:

- 2 cups sassafras root, cleaned and chopped
- 4 cups water
- 1-2 tbsp honey or sugar (optional)
- 1 cinnamon stick (optional)

Instructions:

1. Bring water to a boil in a pot.
2. Add chopped sassafras root and reduce heat.
3. Simmer for 15-20 minutes until the water turns deep red.
4. Strain out the roots and sweeten with honey or sugar.
5. Serve warm or chilled over ice.

Wild Ginger Syrup

Ingredients:

- 1 cup wild ginger root, sliced
- 2 cups water
- 1 cup honey or sugar

Instructions:

1. Simmer wild ginger root in water for 20 minutes.
2. Strain and return liquid to heat.
3. Stir in honey/sugar and simmer until syrup thickens.
4. Store in a jar and use for tea, cocktails, or desserts.

Yarrow Infused Oil

Ingredients:

- 1 cup fresh yarrow flowers and leaves
- 1 cup olive oil

Instructions:

1. Place yarrow in a clean jar.
2. Pour olive oil over and seal the jar.
3. Let infuse in a sunny spot for 2-4 weeks.
4. Strain and store in a dark bottle.
5. Use for skin healing or massage oil.

Chickweed Pesto

Ingredients:

- 2 cups fresh chickweed
- ½ cup nuts (pine nuts, walnuts, or almonds)
- ½ cup Parmesan cheese
- 2 cloves garlic
- ½ cup olive oil
- Salt and black pepper, to taste

Instructions:

1. Blend chickweed, nuts, Parmesan, and garlic.
2. Slowly add olive oil while blending.
3. Season with salt and pepper.
4. Serve with pasta, bread, or as a dip.

Miner's Lettuce Salad

Ingredients:

- 4 cups fresh miner's lettuce
- ½ cup cherry tomatoes, halved
- ¼ cup red onion, thinly sliced
- ¼ cup crumbled feta cheese
- 2 tbsp olive oil
- 1 tbsp lemon juice
- Salt and black pepper, to taste

Instructions:

1. Rinse and dry miner's lettuce.
2. Toss with cherry tomatoes and red onion.
3. Drizzle with olive oil and lemon juice.
4. Season with salt and pepper.
5. Sprinkle with feta cheese and serve.

Watercress Soup

Ingredients:

- 2 cups fresh watercress
- 1 onion, chopped
- 2 cloves garlic, minced
- 2 cups vegetable or chicken broth
- 1 cup heavy cream or coconut milk
- 2 tbsp butter
- Salt and black pepper, to taste

Instructions:

1. Sauté onion and garlic in butter until soft.
2. Add broth and bring to a simmer.
3. Stir in watercress and cook for 5 minutes.
4. Blend until smooth and return to heat.
5. Stir in cream, season with salt and pepper, and serve warm.

Thistle Root Stir-Fry

Ingredients:

- 2 cups thistle root, peeled and sliced
- 1 tbsp soy sauce
- 1 tbsp sesame oil
- 1 clove garlic, minced
- ½ tsp ginger, grated
- 1 green onion, chopped

Instructions:

1. Rinse and peel thistle root, then slice into thin pieces.
2. Heat sesame oil in a pan and sauté garlic and ginger.
3. Add thistle root and stir-fry for 5 minutes.
4. Drizzle with soy sauce and mix well.
5. Garnish with green onions and serve.

Cactus Fruit (Prickly Pear) Sorbet

Ingredients:

- 4 ripe prickly pears
- ½ cup sugar or honey
- 1 cup water
- 1 tbsp lime juice

Instructions:

1. Peel and blend prickly pears, then strain to remove seeds.
2. In a saucepan, dissolve sugar in water over low heat.
3. Combine with prickly pear juice and lime juice.
4. Chill the mixture, then churn in an ice cream maker.
5. Freeze for 2 hours and serve.

Wild Mustard Greens Sauté

Ingredients:

- 2 cups wild mustard greens
- 1 tbsp olive oil
- 2 cloves garlic, minced
- ½ tsp red pepper flakes
- Salt and black pepper, to taste

Instructions:

1. Rinse and chop mustard greens.
2. Heat olive oil in a pan and sauté garlic until fragrant.
3. Add greens and red pepper flakes, cooking for 3 minutes.
4. Season with salt and pepper.
5. Serve as a side dish or over rice.

Wild Asparagus with Lemon Butter

Ingredients:

- 1 bunch wild asparagus
- 2 tbsp butter
- 1 tbsp lemon juice
- ½ tsp salt
- Black pepper, to taste

Instructions:

1. Trim tough ends of wild asparagus.
2. Steam or blanch for 2-3 minutes until tender.
3. Melt butter and mix with lemon juice.
4. Drizzle over asparagus and season with salt and pepper.
5. Serve warm.

Indian Cucumber Root & Herb Salad

Ingredients:

- 1 cup Indian cucumber root, sliced thin
- 1 cup mixed greens
- ½ cup cucumber, diced
- ¼ cup fresh herbs (mint, dill, or basil)
- 2 tbsp olive oil
- 1 tbsp apple cider vinegar
- Salt and black pepper, to taste

Instructions:

1. Rinse and slice Indian cucumber root.
2. Toss with greens, cucumber, and herbs.
3. Drizzle with olive oil and vinegar.
4. Season with salt and pepper.
5. Serve chilled.

www.ingramcontent.com/pod-product-compliance
Lightning Source LLC
LaVergne TN
LVHW081507060526
838201LV00056BA/2982